After Brockman

After Brockman

JAY BAIL
JEFF BERNER
MAGDA CORDELL
IRA EINHORN
HUGH FOX
JOHN HACKETT
DAN ISAAC
DOUGLAS KELLEY
RICHARD KOSTELANETZ
PAUL A. LEE

JOHN C. LILLY
JOHN McHALE
RICHARD MORRIS
MICHAEL PERKINS
R.S. PICCIOTTO
BERN PORTER
EDWIN SCHLOSSBERG
ALAN SONDHEIM
GERD STERN
HEINZ VON FOERSTER

A Symposium

ABYSS PUBLICATIONS

1974

For
Katinka Matson

ISBN: 0-911856-14-5

ISSN: 0001-3722

ABYSS, Vol. 4, Nos. 1 - 3

This publication was partially funded by a grant from
the Coordinating Council of Literary Magazines.

Technical assistance by Stephen Barr

Cover Photo by Maureen Lambray

TABLE OF CONTENTS

THE CONTRIBUTORS

JAY BAIL, novelist and critic, is editor and publisher of *Book Magazine,* which he formerly published as *The San Francisco Book Review.*

JEFF BERNER, author and photographer, directs the Innerspace Project in Mill Valley, California. His books include *The Innerspace Project* (1972) and *The Photographic Experience* (1974).

IRA EINHORN is a poet concerned with the paradigms of new technologies. He lives and works in Philadelphia and is the author of *78-187880* (1972).

HUGH FOX is Associate Professor in the Department of American Thought and Language, Michigan State University, Ph.D. from the University of Illinois, twice Fulbright Professor of American Studies in Latin America. He is editor of *Ghost Dance: The International Quarterly of Experimental Poetry.*

JOHN HACKETT, Assistant Professor of English at Wesleyan University, received a Ph.D. in Classical Studies from St. Louis University. At Wesleyan, he has been Master of East College and a Fellow at the Center for the Humanities.

Rabbi **DAN ISAAC** received a Master of Hebrew Letters degree from Hebrew Union College in 1957 and a Ph.D. in English Literature from the University of Chicago in 1968. He now lives in New York where he is a theater critic, Literary Advisor to the Circle-In-The-Square, and Assistant Professor of English at Manhattanville College.

DOUGLAS KELLEY is a mathematician who lives and works in Chicago.

RICHARD KOSTELANETZ, critic and social historian, has authored and edited many books including *The Theater of Mixed Means* (1968), *Master Minds* (1969), *Visual Language* (1970), *Metamorphosis In The Arts* (1971), *Human Alternatives* (1971), *Social Speculations* (1971), and *Breakthrough Fictioneers* (1973).

PAUL A. LEE is Executive Director of the William James Association in Santa Cruz, California. Dr. Lee, a former Chaplain of Brandeis University, has been a faculty member of Harvard, M.I.T., and University of California, Santa Cruz.

JOHN C. LILLY, M.D. is a scientist, psychiatrist, and explorer of inner spaces. His books include *Man and Dolphin* (1961), *Programming and Metaprogramming in the Human Biocomputer* (1972), and *Center of the Cyclone* (1972). He is currently conducting experiments with isolation water tanks in Malibu, California.

JOHN McHALE and **MAGDA CORDELL** live in Vestal, New York. Ms. Cordell is a painter and Research Associate of the Center for Integrative Studies, State University of New York at Binghamton. Dr. McHale is an artist/sociologist, and Director of the Center. His books include *The Future of the Future* (1969), *The Ecological Context* (1971), and *World Facts and Trends* (1972).

RICHARD MORRIS, poet and critic, lives in San Francisco. He is the editor and publisher of *Camel's Coming Newsletter* and Coordinator of COSMEP (Committee of Small Magazine Editors and Publishers).

MICHAEL PERKINS, novelist and critic, lives in Woodstock, New York. Among other projects, he edited and published *Down Here,* co-founded and served as editor-in-chief of Croton Press, and was book critic of the *Los Angeles Free Press.* He has published nine novels.

R.S. PICCIOTTO is Associate Professor of Romance Languages at Queens College where he also serves as Assistant Dean of Faculty for the School of International Education.

BERN PORTER is a physicist, publisher and author who now lives in Maine. His more recent works include *The Wastemaker* (1972) and *The Manhattan Telephone Book* (1974).

EDWIN SCHLOSSBERG received a Ph.D. in Science and Literature from Columbia University. He has been a teaching fellow in the Design Department of Southern Illinois University, a lecturer at the Columbia School of Architecture in New York, and director with

R. Buckminster Fuller of the World Game research project in New York. His books include *Einstein and Beckett* (1972).

ALAN SONDHEIM is an artist and philosopher. He has been a lecturer at Rhode Island School of Design, and a guest lecturer at Nova Scotia College of Art and Design and Newcastle Polytechnic.

GERD STERN is a poet and artist. He has been Associate Professor at Harvard Graduate School in Education, visiting professor in the History of Consciousness Program at University of California at Santa Cruz, and is presently the President of Intermedia Systems, Inc. His books of poetry include *Afterimages* (1965).

HEINZ VON FOERSTER is the Director of the Biological Computer Laboratory of the University of Illinois. Born in Vienna in 1911, he received a Ph.D. in Physics from the University Breslau. He has been Chairman of the Committee for Cognitive Studies, University of Illinois; President, the Wenner-Gren Foundation for Anthropological Research; Chairman of the Board of Directors of the Cybernetics Research Institute; and Chairman of the Research Board and member of the Board of Directors of the American Society for Cybernetics. He is the editor of *Principles of Self-Organization* (1962), and *Purposive Systems* (1968) as well as the author of scores of papers and scholarly articles.

THE END OF PHILOSOPHY:
ON JOHN BROCKMAN

by Jay Bail

1

There are certain writers whose thought is so important that it doesn't matter whether you agree with them or not. A verbal tension so powerful, an ascetic appetite so huge and consuming forces us both to accept the vision as a revelation and to resist it as a duty.

John Brockman's *Afterwords* (Anchor, $3.50) has recently been published. Composed of three separate works, two of which have appeared in somewhat altered form, *Afterwords* deserves to be read and experienced as few books do in these times of informational overload.

For John Brockman is the kind of writer you both agree with and don't agree with at all. Either way you must pay a profound attention to what he says in this remarkable book. In short, sharp strokes of words, he breaks through the very forest of meaning by denying meaning, eschewing traditional forms of activities, thoughts and emotions. It is not what he says that is so valuable; *it is his whole manner of negating what can be said.* His words backtrack on themselves, stalk their own meanings, and thrash about in the underbrush of our sensibilities. There is a total devastation of language, isolating and withering the very hands our dreams are made of.

Artaud might stumble out of his frenzied asylum to shake the chaotic hand of Brockman. Wittgenstein might pause a moment, sit up from his numerous notebooks (ah so ah yes) into the square root of minus *Afterwords*. And even Dostoyevsky, poor scoundrel, lost in the wilderness of his vows, might honor Brockman by asking him for a small loan.

2

An incredible chaos of Brockman is the source of both agreement and disagreement. For if chaos exists, does this reality also exist? Brockman says no. If we agree that man, amid his words, thoughts, constructions is faceless, nameless, beingless, then shall we also accept purpose and drive and love?

Brockman says no.

If nothing but words exist, do we?

3

Brockman says no.

Things. The tightrope of unimpeachable triviality.

Things. They caress and fondle, soothe and warm, and then finally burst into more things, more events, words, smiles, emotions, and handwavings. You can't lift a conception without things invading in hordes. And always the things make sense, there is a reason for their being, a purpose to their face. And yet...

Things. Their self-righteous inescapability - an illusion. Events, places, hands, words are knots of tenuous existence that, if untied will reveal nothing, a void, an is-ness. Do not believe what is in front of your mind - it is not real, nor is your mind. These bonds of love, those of envy, that of man, and this of child - all gone, lost in the whorl of happenstance. Man is dead, traditional gatherings of entity-patterns are dissolved, and the universe is not real. It simply *is*. Any description will deaden, delimit, decrease the actual existence. It simply *is*.

4

A half-century of art, caught in things. And more things.
Covering like moss. A living theatre celebrating the arbitrary,
the minutiae of taste. Novels avalanching over our certainties
with the grime of inconsequentiality. Painting as a Great Reveler,
the splash of liquid on canvas, the rampage of formlessness, the
feast of the grotesque.

(A series of timeless tableaus, Brockman writes, *an infinitely
successive series of nows. But this can't be. It isn't. A picture held us captive. And we could not get outside it, for it
lay in our language and language seemed to repeat it to us in-
exorably. We are free from the pictures and the lives lived in
the mind are at an end.)*

To examine words minutely is to break the back of verbal
meaning, destroying the moving form in a perfect ease of
shattered bodies. To dissemble intellectually is to destroy the
whole, to be lost among the fibers of organic isolation.
Never forget the wholeness you started from, the values and
constructions you dissected in the name of investiture. Always remember that a taking-apart implies a putting-to-
gether or else you will be lost in the high drift of chance.

5

There is no one writing like John Brockman. To agree with
him is to realize his value in dissecting, destroying, revealing
the certainty behind uncertainty behind certainty.

To disagree with Brockman is to still realize the value of de-
molition. For if there is nothingness, and if there is something-
ness, then to realize the first is to resurrect the importance of
the second. And in the last, the first was born; and at the first
we shall discover the last.

(Replace all words pertaining to ownership with words concerning functions, operations . . .
Consciousness does not exist; indeed, there is no reason to believe that it ever did exist.)

(The perception of a signal happens 'now' but its impulse happened then. The present instant is the plane upon which the signals of all being are projected. This instant, the interval, constitutes all that is directly experienced . . . The interpretation of the ordering of the brain takes place while new ordering is continually happening.. It is almost as though there were two parallel planes.)

There are two parallel planes that cut across differing reality levels. One (interpretation) has to do with continuity, cause-and-effect, time, space - and conscious will. The other (chaos) involves drift, abruptness, frozen shards of time - and arbitrary whim. The first entails a whole world of conceptualization and an endless range of possibilities. The second is eerie, hollow, frozen to a perpetual is-ness, utterly non-human. Yet from another standpoint, this chaos is the life-giver from which all possibilities flow, the infinite present, the undying atomic particles, the sound of one hand clapping.

Any phenomenon must be considered through the bifocality of both element and entity. To understand the significance of the whole entity without a knowledge of the elemental components is incomplete. Seeing the components without evaluating the characteristics of the entity to which they belong is likewise incomplete. One leads to a sterile consideration of values without any means of application or, indeed, a fitting knowledge of what events these values shall apply to. The other leads to utter randomness without any knowledge of meaning, or the means toward meaning - coherent intellect.

This randomness is what Brockman - and a good deal of western thought - considers as direct experience. But what does 'direct' mean? Why do we so willingly go out of our minds to come to our senses, presumably the seat of The Direct Experience? Why is *that* direct and thought not? Why should we see the interpretive capability of the mind considered as a block to Reality, a filter through which only part of The Truth seeps in? A Direct Experience means beyond doubt, means certain; while something discovered through rationality is considered imperfect, uncertain. Therefore, what is certain and perfect must be true because we do not doubt it. Truth then becomes the certainty of convenience, the inability to doubt.

And since to doubt implies falseness, anything capable of doubt must be incomplete and false. The mind only is capable of doubt, and man's distinguishing humanistic characteristic is his mind; therefore, man is false, dead, a cardboard sign in a vacant lot.

And so, to know through intelligence becomes a knowing through falseness. To know through not-intelligence becomes true. 'Directly experienced' means not open to question, a tyranny of truth, an incommunicable sameness.

The faith of the gods rests on their inability to speak. Their holiness springs from a fountain of matchless stupidity.

8

(The difference between human experience and neural experience is the difference between illusion and reality, between choice and no choice . . . The ordering and arrangement are a continual functional happening. The ordering and arrangement are all happening. The ordering and arranging are all that is actually happening. Nothing else ever happens.)

(Navigate through reality with no pretense of knowledge. The unity is methodological. The unity is in the activity and will not

lead to any final answer. It is a path. All paths are the same;
they lead nowhere. Keep moving . . . Not sex, not unconscious
urges, not iconic archetypes, not metaphysics. There is no purpose.
There are no goals.)

9

There are no goals. If you say so. If you wait for the
Godot of your values, if purpose must somehow invade you
with the certainty of its presence - then nothing will happen.
For there *is* nothing but a swarm of neuron happenings, intervals, methodological patterns. Brockman is totally correct
throughout. There is no purpose.

But why not make some purpose? Life does not exist in the
body of a tortured god but in the hands of your own will to
elaborate. There are no goals except the sense of your own
crucifixion *towards.*

10

(What must be analyzed is the process, the operant concept
of what something is doing, rather than static, fixed states of
being . . . The information that was received without consent
or awareness. The notion of free man, the notion of individual
choice, is no longer valid.)

11

Realization of chaos calls forth varying attitudes to life,
based on three fundamental premises: (1) the reality of only drift;
(2) the reality of only purpose; (3) the reality of both drift and
purpose.

Challenge lies in overcoming the impossible, riding the daylight
down. If it is true that man is simply a product of physiological
functioning, organic patterns of entity, and that there is no free
choice - then he ought to attempt to create some, to write on water.
To do, in whatever realm of being, is precisely the challenge *because*
it is impossible. For truth is the challenge of the impossible as

well as the inertia of the probable. Which step you take - towards the impossible or into the probable - is the measure of one's thrust to life. The first is *always,* the other is the *never-having-been.* The first is never being because it is about to become. The other is never being because it has always been. One is the future, the other the past. Hence, is-ness, neural experience becomes the present, mindless, blurred widow of chance.

It is impossible to be conscious without an attempt to kill the sky.

12

(There is no continuity, no accretion, no incremental serial advances, no depth. There is no nature. There was never anyone but me talking to me of me. No nature: just a nature created in what it says.)

Words are simply one stage of a single line of development within a vast urge to elaboration - (which includes other lines, such as vision, taste, touch). This urge drives right through words to merge into concepts and systems of conceptualizations. These systems are as different from individual words as a human being is from an individual cell. To refer to the human being as nothing but cells - and thereby dismiss consciousness - is to miss a vast complexity that is particularly human. To choose to ignore systems of conceptualization, as Brockman does, and to consider individual words alone as true, as Brockman does, is not to accomodate the different and quite unique entity that is a system of conceptualization. It is to avoid a complexity so vast that it has become a simple, new organism, unifying its properties to deal with the range of its increased potentiality.

Systems of conceptualization have a validity of their own. They do not depend totally on words. While they may cease to exist if all words should stop, it is equally true that when concepts stop, all words will also come to an end. For words that are not part of something are part of nothing, and words that are part of nothing become nothing themselves.

Both words and systems of conceptualization are real and both are vital. To deny one is, in essence, to deny the other. You cannot ignore rungs without changing a ladder into mere pieces of wood. You cannot take cells or words and say that they are truer than humans or systems of conceptualization. They are neither truer nor falser. *They are the same as.* Both are simply one stage in an irresistible hurtle toward complexity. But the other stages could not exist without it and it could not exist without the other stages.

13

(The author presents not ideas, but information. Not words and images, but a transaction that can be measured only in terms of information . . . It is a question of searching for questions. It is an attempt to create a working model, not with an eye to truth but to convenience. The only rules applicable are those that are convenient to use. We move toward an always inferred, unknowable reality.)

(Experience a minute. Experience an hour. Can you experience a minute and an hour together, simultaneously, at the same time? This is an important question to ask.)

14

And the void is a concept, just as something is a concept. There is no reality but reality.

(The universe is finite: there is nothing beyond, nothing outside this finiteness. Just the next measurement, the next word.)

We create with words but we cannot uncreate through words. For there is no uncreation. There is no void. There is only continuous existence at different pitches of necessity. It is impossible to stop being. We cannot be certain that we were ever *not* or will be *not* since all our conceptualization of *not* are symbols of systems of purposive relationships. That they may refer by a congruence of functionality to an empirical fact is simply another system of purpcsive relationship. All that we can be sure of is that we are a maze of purposive relationships in a mirror of symbols.

It is impossible to die or be born since we are alive and to image the piles of increments (or the lack of them) that we refer to as birth (or death) is simply another purposive relationship within a mirror of symbols.

If death is the end of all, including purposive relationships, it is impossible to understand this within the ceaseless purpose of relationships. If death entails another reality level, it is impossible to understand this since we cannot take into account the variable functions of this vastly pitched system of purposive elaboration. We cannot know death because (a) it is nothing, or (b) it is everything.

15

(Finite man, finite intelligence: control. Not in control, but as control, as reality, as intelligence. Finite intelligence: the mass is no greater than the singular man of the mass. Expect no life from the mass. Expect no voice from the people.)

(No sign of life but life, itself, the presence of the intelligible in that which is created as its symbol. Life is a knowledge, not an existence. Life is not lived, it is known, Known: not experienced. Imagine, you had an experience.)

16

Brockman is hardly a discursive writer. He does not reason from a premise to a conclusion but rather starts with a conclusion (the utter reality of words) and topples backward to several premises that may fit. Nor is the *what,* the content of his books of that much importance.

Brockman's value is nothing less than a violent *incursion* against meaning and, ultimately, against the whole concept of human. He pierces you with the sharpness of his abstentions to conjoin. As in a play or a novel, he does not tell you but shows you. He shows you by breaking all conceptual patterns. Short sentences butchered of a possible fullness of verbs, adverbs and adjectives. Disjunctive sentences falling over one another in a totalitarian isolation. Short paragraphs and chapters that chop off any attempt to expound, extrapolate, explain, excuse. There is no one writing like John Brockman because Brockman writes with the total brutality of an executioner who shows you how to make peace before he hangs your participles. And you make peace, you come to rest in the flux of words through a sophisticated ignorance, a purposeful amnesia of meaning. You must follow Brockman down all the blind alleys to understand and to experience the totality of negation.

Brockman is important because, while you do not fully agree with him, he has force-fed you the chaos of the particle. And the man who has been in the depths of the particle comes to the surface of meaning fresh, with the knowledge of the workability of life, with an abundance of chaos lived. And he will know the relative and utter necessity of being human.

For the chaos of the word exists always, while the meaning of the word is always new. Both are profound truths that together form the blood and the skin of this incredible wash of life.

ABOUT PART I OF *AFTERWORDS*

by Jeff Berner

Brockman is a theoretical physicist of consciousness who has imploded the idea of Man, leaving the emperor naked. The emperor of self-reflexive consciousness. In "Commentary on *The Secret of the Golden Flower,*" from 1931, Jung pointed to the fact that Western man has been blinded by his fascination with consciousness itself.

I'm responding here to just the first 102 pages of *Afterwords,* being a revision of *By the Late John Brockman.* Material in quotes is from Brockman, and the rest is either condensed and paraphrased, or my own comments.

"Man is dead." Words and concepts are hand-me-down belief-capsules. Abstractions are biases. We have an outside chance to go from *I seem to be* (a thing, an animal, a man), to *I seem to be a verb.* The nervous system is a tiny keyhole through which info slips into human awareness. Reality for humankind has been millennia of *deja vu.* Man, the time-binder (and so proud of it!), alienates himself from Now with this special gift. His consciousness is an echo-chamber. "Man, an instant too old to exist." Meanings, ideas, are material flotsam compared with the dance of processing information and responding to that info. Information is just impulses until decoded and read by the brain. This means filtered, interpreted, nay *given* meaning or content by the receiver. All info is bias propaganda and belief-system attachment. Only the process of universe is of amazing grace interest. The choice-function itself, in man, is a conceptual illusion.

Adam's bite into the apple strudel was the moment he concepted himself; self-reflexion was The Fall. Man has had millennia modeling himself as a technique of being, and this "cultural heritage" is obsolete at this point. For Brockman, philosophy is a critique of all abstractions in the lexicon of consciousness. "Only by renouncing an explanation of life in the ordinary sense do we gain a possibility of taking into account its characteristics." That perception harmonizes with ancient Sufi teaching techniques. The seed has been there a long time, this seed of imploding consciousness.

To the self-attached man, the monkey digging his own reflection in the funhouse mirror, life is bubbling with meanings: His insatiable gestalt mechanism takes a vast field and sucks out tolerable elements, makes apparent order out of apparent chaos, decorating the void with ideas, feelings, politics, etc. This decoration, information, is a measure of effect. "Start with effect and work backward." We are now invited to give ourselves up as a race, in the manner that the East invites the individual to give up his ego. "The evolutionary significance of all this is unbelievable, for man. It is the end of importance. It is the end of man."

The media wraparound upped the ante of man's attachment, by adding the extra satisfaction of electrical pulses. TV, for example, not only carries images of violence, but is itself doing (did) electro-neurological violence upon the eye/brain. Man became the monkey banging the bar which sent the juice through the electrodes which gave him orgasms. Process is supreme over content. The brain as echo chamber and reducing valve, channels *what is* through the filter of *what was*. Mere matching. We can now make a leap to "Observation and measurement, no classification and categorization," but this leap is the most risky, painful sort of adventure, since "Perhaps the death of an abstraction is the most difficult death." The obstinacy of self-authenticating consciousness derives from the essential fact that "For the brain, there is no illusion." Only bias-invested value systems shout at one another, *fraud, fraud!* And whole nations slaughter the mortal flesh to defend their attachments to abstractions.

Man was man-made. If evolution is to go beyond the Uroboros stage, he will discover the art of deciphering neural codes, to explode his habit of building the same towers out of the same alphabet blocks. Thus, cracking the code may crack the cosmic egg. As a prisoner of his biophysical functions, man's notion of freedom has been an absurd conceptual, arrogant, fantasy. "Language. This exercise is using language to say that language does not exist." Better to say, for the moment, that language is becoming obsolete. Innerspace travel is more hazardous, more "important" than the Newtonian locomotive trips to outerspace.

Brockman's *Man is dead* imperative is destructive in the way that Zen scrapes away romanticism, in the way that existentialism explodes values, in the manner that Sufism laughs at millennia of human pretense.

My own heart-biases incline me to leave this writing with a thought from Hazrat Inayat Khan: *Renunciation is always for a purpose: it is to kindle the soul that nothing may hold it back from God; but when it is kindled, the life of renunciation is not necessary.*

If man could get beyond his lust for eating food, eating ideas, and eating each other, he could truly die. But at this instant of past/present/future, man isn't dead yet. But caught in the moldy costumes of historical drama, we have a strong impression that we are utterly marooned in the twentieth century.

KOHOUTEK IS COMING

by Ira Einhorn

EDGES OF ABRASION
BEYOND THE FEALTY OF WORDS

A   F   T   E   R   W   O   R   D   S

INTEGRATED SUMMATION
OF OUR PSUEDOPODS
MENTAL PROBES
INTO THE UNKNOWN OF THE FUTURE
THE CUTTING EDGE OF KNOWLEDGE
COLDLY LAID OUT
           P H
            O E   TABLE OF WHITE
            N   O
                              R U R
PRINT
  EADING
    Y
      E
       S TO DEVOUR
A SUMMA OF THE DISSENTING VOICES
WHOSE WORDS
CARRY US BEYOND
THE PRESENT STRUCTURE
OF OUR DESSICATED BEING
MAN IS DEAD
THE HUBRIS OF HUMANISM
ONLY
          A DARK SHADOW
THAT HAUNTS
OUR CANCEROUS MODES OF AUTHORITY
WHOSE FORMS

CLOG THE NECESSARY PATHWAYS
THAT WILL PROVIDE
THIS BLUE PLANET
WITH THE POSSIBILITY
OF A FUTURE

OUR HUMANISTIC ABSTRACTIONS
GONE
WE STAND
IN THE FACE OF
THE CLEAR POSSIBILITIES
OF INFORMATION

AFRAID
ALONE
IN A WORLD
DEVOID OF SHADOW

THE CLARITY OF PROCESS
FLOWING ABOUT
IN THE MAGNETIC SPACE
OF DE CHIRICO
DRAWN
BY OUR HABITS
TO THE BRUTAL PURGATIONS
OF ARTAUD
CLINGING DESPERATELY
TO ANY MODE
WHOSE ABSTRACTION
RELIEVES THE TENSION
OF CONFRONTATION
WHOSE STRESS
CREATES SPECIES OF ACTION
THAT FILL OUR MEDIA
WITH A DISTENSION
APOCALYPTIC IN ITS AGONY

A F T E R   W O R D S

A BRIDGE
HELIX—LIKE
IN ITS INTERTWINED GATHERING

OF WORDS
THAT ENZYMATICALLY
REGULATE
THE MOVEMENT TOWARD THE NEW
HOSTAGES
TO THE BINDS
THAT WE USE
TO COSSET OUR MINDS
WE STRUGGLE
TO TRANSFORM
OUR BROKEN INSTRUMENTS
INTO
    A
     PROCESS
         OF
           TRANSFORMATION
THAT
    WILL ONCE AGAIN
ALLOW
    ESSENCE TO EMERGE
FROM THE TATTERED RUINS
OF THIS BODY
WHOSE PERSONAL OWNERSHIP
IS IN CONFUSION

DARK PLAIN OF EARTH
LITTERED
WITH THE REIFIED ASPECTS
OF ABSTRACTION
THAT NO LONGER HAVE A PURPOSE
TERMINAL SEWAGE
THAT MUST BE REPROCESSED
BY A
COHERENT ECOLOGY OF MIND
THAT FUNCTIONS
AT THE CROSSROADS OF
BETWEEN
ATOM
    AND
      UNIVERSE
AS
A SHUNTING DEVICE

SORTING AND SEPARATING
IN THE MIDST OF
A FLOW
THAT IS CONTINUOUS AND ETERNAL

EARTHED BY THIS UNDERSTANDING
OF PROCESS
WE CAN MOVE INTO
NEW REALMS OF ABSTRACTION
EXTENDING
OUR REACH
ENABLING
OUR BEING
TO EMPOWER
SPECIES
WITH
FORMS
THAT CARRY US BEYOND
THE CRUCIBLE OF CRISIS
INTO REGIONS
PREVIOUSLY UNKNOWN
COSMOS AGAIN
FILLED
INFORMED
WITH NEW WONDERS
THAT DAILY
FILL THE BLUE SPACE
OF OUR SKIES
WITH PROMISE
OF GALACTIC CONNECTION
IF WE COULD ONLY
BREAKDOWN
       U
       T
OF OUR PRESENT ABSTRACTIONS
THAT DISALLOW
THE TRIPARTATE
EMERGENCE
              OF
            U.F.O.

ELECTROGRAVITICS△URI GELLER

HERE
            IN 1974
                            IN THE BACKWASH
OF
        A   F   T   E   R   W   O   R   D   S

THAT
            SPEAKS SO WELL
OF
U
R   ONE PRESENT REALITY:
        THE FLOW OF INFORMATION
THAT
        IS NOW
                U
                R   ONLY CURRENCY
THAT
        IS NOW

FOR SURVIVAL
IN THE WORLD OF CHAOS
THAT IS OUR PRESENT
                    L
                    A
                    N
                    E   SURROUND
                    T
                    A
                    R
                    Y
NEW MODES OF INFORMATION
THAT CURRENT ABSTRACTION
THAT MIGHT LIFT US
BEYOND THE CHAOS
INTO CONNECTION
WITH THAT GALACTIC FIX
THAT
            WILL PROVIDE US
WITH
            THAT SO NEEDED
SENSE
        OF
            C   O   S   M   O   S

POST-MODERN OLOGIES

by Hugh Fox

1.

Harriet Daimler in *The Organization* (New York, 1971) invents a number of words that are particularly apt to any study of John Brockman:

1. *Phantiverse* - The fantasy-universe in which most of the world lives, consisting of the "old" words/concepts to live by: mother, father, family, love, hate, will, patriotism.

2. *Realomyth* - The entire "content" of 1....in all its ramifications and complexities.

3. *Defactification* - Getting rid of 1 and 2 and replacing it *(subfuging)* with 4.

4. *The Subliminal* - The de-fantisized "real" world.

Brockman's psychology, ontology, sociology, metaphysics and neurology - they're all in *Afterwords* - are about what Harriet Daimler would call "The Subliminal World". He really doesn't concern himself with the "Phantiverse" at all, doesn't "straddle" the Modern and Post-Modern, but *begins* to define from INSIDE THE POST—MODERN PARAMETERS.

Perhaps the beginning of his vision is neurology/cybernetics, the recognition that the Brain, under its historical identity-layers of Religion, Patriotism, Love, Science, Honor, etc. is an *automatic* information-machine. The Judeo-Christian "aura" that we have secreted about the "Human Being" has nothing at all to do with the fact that Man is an Aqueous Machine, that he is limited to what his nervous system itself can do and like all other machines he operates, not on the edge of a metaphysical infinite, but within the confines of definable neurological capabilities:

> *We are beyond space and time; we are beyond good and evil. There is only information. It is the control, the measure by which the operation of the brain changes. There is always complete control.* *(Page 55)*

> *The brain is a terminal machine in the process that is itself the dynamic, the reference point. The reference point is not to be found as a substantial basis, but in consideration of function and operations. It will be found in the process of transmission of neural pattern. It is through observation of operations, measurement of information, that this dynamic situation can be dealt with. Observation and measurement, not classification and categorization.* *(Page 73)*

Afterwords is literally a book *after* words. Words represent *the* major wall between Man and Reality. Reality is "out there," but between Man and Out There there is a whole pseudo-world *(phantiverse)* of words/concepts that blocks any possible understanding of the Out There in itself. We exist in a "finite world of words," (Page 221) but the world Out There is "unintelligible. . . we feel the absurdity of an order, a whole, a knowledge, that which arranged the rendezvous, within its vital boundary, in the mind." (Page 227)

The best, the *most* we can do is get out of our minds/words/ concepts and immerse ourselves as thoroughly as possible in the Pure Out There: "Crashing through the personal psychic walls. I am out of my mind . . . the lives lived in the mind are at an end. They never were." (p. 243) Only after we do divest ourselves of our historical, religious, cultural LOAD, after we confront the fact that all our glorious concepts and goals are little wet cellular transactions, that that's *all* we are is the Neurological Machine, Brockman does not offer us any kind of salvation. *All* he offers, in fact, is a liberation into confusion, uncertainty, enigma, obfuscation. He is not a Witness to a new Religion of the Freed Mind, but rather a cicerone who conducts his sightseers into EMPTINESS. Beyond is merely more beyond:

> *Man is dead: the great explainer, the great*
> *explanation. He has lost the center: he was the*
> *center, the whole in which he was contained.*
> *There can be no more explanations, no more*
> *worlds.   (Page 263)*

> *Nobody knows, and you can't find out.*
> *(Page 292)*

We get rid of our usual way of thinking about our brain and senses.
There aren't any "pictures" or "feelings" or "smells" in our brain -
our total reality-perception is based on receptor mechanisms, limited,
controlled, determined by the nature and range of the receptors.
Which eliminates the validity of the World in our Head compared
to the World Around us. This is the Perception-Destruct Mechanism.
Stage one. In Stage two, Brockman eliminates our Word-World,
the comfortable retreat into Abstractions that give us direction and
meaning. So we toss them out too. We become wordless neurological Things. We try to merge into raw reality . . . but we can't
. . . and that's where Brockman leaves us hanging.

2.

Afterwords assimilates and uses the writings by authors like
Whitehead, Kubler, Whorf, Niels Bohr, Rene Dubos, Carlos
Castenadas, Heisenberg, Sir James Jeans, Wittgenstein, Buckminster
Fuller, Eddington, Bertrand Russell, T.E. Hulme and T.S. Eliot.

At the same time the message is a kind of massive, corporate
summing up of the Head Mystique of the 1960's. I remember toward the end of the 60's attending a Leary Light-Show/Guru Pitch
at the Santa Monica auditorium that essentially was about losing
the Ego in the Cosmos, getting rid of our "normally"/traditionally-
conditioned senses and language-usage and supra-sensorily, passing
the senses, finding self in the genetic-cosmic pool inside us, word-
lessly merging with Reality IN ITSELF. It was Heidegger's Being
in Time turned into an Operational Reality.

This was the Haight-Ashbury Message, the Berkeley Message of

Charlie Potts, J.O. Simon, Richard Krech . . . it was the reality I *lived* between 1960-1970: I was a Cosmic Zero, whatever I'd been trained to believe was "out there" *wasn't* out there. *In order to even approach* the Out There I had to discard my whole trained, dyed-in-occidental-dead-head civilization Past.

So Brockman's message is the Hippy Message, the *real* Hippy Message that fastened on American (and East) Indian Shamanism, Peyote Visions, Behavior-unconditioning Light Shows and Pot, *anything* to destroy the Judeo-Christian-Scientific-Industrial-Perception-Cage . . . only it's also the message of the Scientific-Philosophical-Psychological Community of Seers. Why this congruence?

A short quote from Bede's *Ecclesiastical History of the English Nation* (completed in 731). Subject - the conversion of pagan, Anglo-Saxon England to Christianity. One of King Edwin's councilors is talking to the King:

Such appears to me, King, this present life of man on earth in comparison with the time which is unknown to us, as though you were sitting at the banquet with your leaders and thanes in winter and the fire was lighted and your hall warmed, and it rained and snowed and stormed outside; and there should come a sparrow and quickly fly through the house, come in through one door and go out through the other. Now in the time that he is inside he is not touched by the storm of winter; but that is only the twinkling of an eye and the least interval, and at once he comes from winter back to winter again. So this life of men appears save for but a little while; what goes before or what follows after we do not know. Therefore, if this teaching should bring anything more certain and more proper, it is fitting that we follow it.

Christianity introduces Graeco-Roman Rationalism into the Shamanistic tribal magic of the Anglo-Saxon world. The herbal, witchcrafting, rune and rhyme spook-world of the Pagan is systematized into an Aristotelean-Platonic-Dying God system which takes the Greek First Cause and turns it into God the Father, takes the Neo-Platonic "oversoul" and creates a Son and Holy Spirit. It is non-proven except in a METAPHYSICAL sense . . . and it continues on almost a thousand years. Man in the Unperceivable

Unknown (the "primitive," Hippy and Brockman view) becomes Man in the Unperceivable Known.

The Cartesian-Baconian Revolution (we are now in the early 1600's almost a thousand years after Bede) was the beginning of a clean sweeping out of "Mind-Idols," a discarding of the Medieval Unperceivable Known and attempt to substitute in its place a Perceivable Known. This attempt to create a Perceivable Known Rationale is the beginning of the Age of Reason, the Rise of Modern Science, Nationalism, Capitalism, the Rights of Man, etc. . . and it deflates and is abandoned at the beginning of the Twentieth century when we turn back to the pagan Anglo-Saxon Charm World again. The multiple "isms" that arise in Europe at the end of the Nineteenth century are basically first an attempt to get rid of the *Abstract* System of Judeo-Christianity not merely in its religious but also in its secular world view (Gauguin, Van Gogh, Maurice Denis, Redon, etc.), then once out of this Abstractionism an attempt to explore Inner Man (Matisse, Henri Rousseau, Nolde, Kandinsky, Kokoschka), then an attempt to *twist* External Reality into a kind of Neo-Abstractionism, a secularized post-Christian religion of Pure Order and Form (Max Jacob, Picasso, Metzinger, Braque), an attempt to let the Magic Self take over (Breton, Dali, de Chirico). . . with Dada in a sense pointing the way toward the Dominant Future, the future of Leary - and Brockman.

As Kurt Schwitters says in *Merz* (1921):

> We are often told that we are incoherent,
> but into the word people try to put an
> insult that is rather hard for me to fathom.
> Everything is incoherent . . . The acts of
> life have no beginning or end. Everything
> happens in a completely idiotic way . . .

When Schwitters talks about Dada being a "disgust with the magnificence of philosophers who for 3000 years have been explaining everything to us . . ." he is ignoring the Anglo-Saxon Magic Interlude and attacking the Greek-Roman-Christianized-Judaic tradition that in a very real sense started *in Greece* as a reaction against the Greek Mystery Religions.

The Brockman World-View is a *scientific, post*-Modern judgment that Man the Unknown is in an Unknown World. There isn't even magic. In the Brockman world there is only Man the Limited Perceiver "lost" in a cosmos of Limited Perceivability.

3.

Brockman's *Afterwords* is the first comprehensive post-modern *Primer,* the only book to date which extends a guiding hand back through Modernism to the Pre-Modern where *most* "intellectuals" still live. *Afterwords* represents a practical mode of updating into the *NOW.* It is a book for meditation, carrying back into the cloisters and chewing on them until the cloisters themselves disappear.

NEGATIVE COMPOSITION

by John Hackett

The articulation comes from Pascal, Nietzsche, Wittgenstein, the bricolage from Brown. Since Brockman admits he's No Man, flowing cape and all, Here Comes Everybody. Recently, he's not himself, he's lost his identity, how else can I put it? Read the headlines, change the channel, how did all these people get into the room?

The structure is commonplace intelligent. A most venerable mudpie the commonplace book, copyright a very recent form of vanity and theft. After the words: Brockman also knows how to read between the lines, to work the crease, to stitch a time and save none. He knows that originality may be pathological. Bad poets imitate, good ones steal. Some allude, the best assimilate verbatim. Here and there Brockman not only reads but also writes between the lines, falls back on his own words. But that will pass, already there are signs. Whole parts of speech now gone.

And save none? Let's see what he says. "Give credit . . . be concerned." "Forget about . . . don't look." "Keep moving . . . ask the fool." Brockman's not afraid to uncle the language along. He becomes what he can scarcely imagine, listen to him scream, a real live moralist. The shift is smooth from is to ought, from catechism to collection plate. So it's not just a commonplace but a courtesy book too. How to survive the flood (why do you want to?). "Let go . . . say no." It's Noah on the sea of bits, and there's a Jonah aboard. Brockman navigates the information tide, negotiates the waves and particles. He pirates the wind, then bags it. Now word me a world if that's not speech I see. More survivals from another millenium. This is the *mundus librarius* of the Middle Ages. It's linear time recycled, neither cycle nor line. Modern culture is medieval spun on the gyre. We come full circle but not to the same place. Genet: we're beyond all that now. Then who's in charge here?

Me says Moebius. No man on the mighty ocean, tacking on the filthy modern tide.

No? No. No? Brockman affirms negation. He knows the power of negative thought is distinctly human. Negentropy is the sum of life in time, the life world as we know it, specifically the sum of human action through history. But man is dead. Negentropy is the most efficient system imaginable for the orderly creation of waste. Negatives shun the light of day, and they shun the underworld as well. There's something all right, but where's nothing? Like nowhere man. Negation does not restrain the life of dreams or the deep structure of sentences or that part of nature which is green. It sits like care in the mind of man. But man is shuffle off this mortal O, he shuffle off to Buffalo, to Bill's defunct rodeo show. Since Brockman's renunciation is complex, here we can only list a few of his sources:

Capt. Nemo,   *Dr. No,*
Nego, no go,   *Mme. Ngo Go,*
Not the girl   *Nowhere Man*
That couldn't say no.   *Or Yoko Ono.*

No man, Otis,   *Nego, nix,*
Nuncle, Joe,   *Nixon, no go,*
The one that couldn't   *Nobodaddy,*
Say it ain't so.   *Pio Nono.*

Save none is the number nine number nine number nine number. To noun is to name is to no. That's not the knowledge. Denounce the noun. There's nothing there. Denounce the noun from 0 to 9. As you would a cantaloupe, to let the cantaloupe occur. Man O man, writes the late author, who comes on now as Gnoman, drowned in his own depths. They have the statistics, but we have the stories.

Snow: There are two cultures. For shame.

Huxley: No go, Percy Snow, don't you know, they're both the same. The sciences and the humanities both use symbols to mediate and control experience, use language to make

sense. Instead, we need a theory and prac-
tice of the immediacies.

Brockman: You guys shuckin' me? (He now
meditates on Godard, runs the movie in his
mind, achieves total loss of affect, and comes
to in the voice of Alpha 60:) *The central
memory is so named because of the primor-
dial role it plays in the logical organization
of Alpha 60. No one has lived in the past.
No one will live in the future. The present
is the form of all life. It is a possession that
no man may wrest from its grasp. Time is
like a circle that turns endlessly. The
descending arc is the past. The arc that
ascends is the future. Everything has been
said . . .*

It remains for me to note how badly the credits are scrambled.
To correct your copy of the *Afterwords* text, read the attributions
in reverse order. A. 1, 2, 3 should be Z. 3, 2, 1, and so on. The
way it stands, all the authorities become impersonators, all the
statements tropes. How did this preposterous editorial blunder
come about? Every schoolboy knows that it's Beckett who com-
plained, "Man will not only prevail, he will endure." And imagine
signing Norbert Wiener's name to "I like it/I don't like it." To
attribute to Hassan the risque conceit from the Vishvassara Tantra,
or to Borges the paradoxical apothegm of Brillouin, smacks of
miching mallecho. One begins to wonder if a force more deliberate
than a printer's devil is to blame, for some of these programmatic
mistakes cast a strange new light on the meaning of familiar sentences. Suppose for instance that it really had been Stevens who
proclaimed, "The words of the world are the life of the world."
Or suppose it had been Ohmann, no Odysseus, who spun the yarn
of how once he descended into the depths and spent the day before he dreamt his death was just a dream, and so was saved,
borne to the surface beneath the stars. Can the common reader
help but stand astonished to read the attribution to Heidegger of
lines that describe the phenomenal world in terms of human ecstasy?
Similarly, the shock of recognition greets the alleged words of
Robbe-Grillet that celebrate the secret heart of things. And so one
comes to see whodunit. Brockman arranged this composition. He
do the police in different voices.

BROCKMAN TRANSCENDING

by Dan Isaac

After reading *Afterwords* by John Brockman, where does one
begin? Better yet, can one begin to talk about a Brockmanian world
where there are only endings?

Let's try a few declarative sentences. The categories Brockman
so despises. But uses nonetheless.

Is *Afterwords* poetry or philosophy? (The questions keep coming.
Maybe after Brockman there are no declarative sentences left.) If it
is poetry, it is clever and occasionally powerful. But the stylistic flaw
sticks out like a sore metaphor. Brockman's poetry is trapped in the
rhetoric of cybernetics. Well then, let's give the category of philosophy
a try. There is a dialectic working here - but it is never Hegelian.
No foundations or syntheses all the way down the line. What is it,
then? Post-Buberian, I believe. Buber argued and lived the I-Thou
relationship, a world of unique relationships always recreating themselves in response to one another. For Brockman there are no relationships. It is an I-Nothing world wearing out.

The best example of Brockmanian dialectics is the following:
On page 236 we read: "No man is my friend. I have no interest in
the human condition. No interest in you, your ideas, your words. No
interest in your opinions." That is all on that page. After that there
is only blank space, a waste of paper, a world of unspoken words.
But on the right hand side of the page opposite we hungrily look for
continuity and completion. Instead of anything like what we are
desperately hoping for, we read: "Don't believe it. Don't believe
anything I say. There's nothing to say. There's nothing to think
about." Suddenly we discover we are in Beckett country: the
dialectics of discontinuity. Consciousness as contradiction.

Is Brockman, then, philosophy or poetry? Why bother with Either/Or? It's Both/And. Plus something insidiously elusive.

Perhaps it is linguistic experimentation after Wittgenstein. After Chomsky. Related to the speech-torture of Peter Handke's very great play, *Kaspar*. Certainly Brockman has invoked the most important linguistic poem in the English language:

The the.

Maybe here we have the best example of Brockman's thought transcending all poetic, philosophic, and linguistic categories. Transcending into nothingness. The futility of the article without an object. The second "the" confronts us with the phenomenon of an article (what is an "article"?) transformed into a meaningless noun. (What is a "noun"?)

All of which brings us to the center of Brockman's endless argument about endings. What is language? What is anything?

But the true power of Brockman's *Afterwords* is none of the above. For all of the above is composed of categories, names. The true power of Brockman is something inexplicably demonic. For he starts me talking to myself. (And even now I hear his mocking voice cry out: What self? There is no self. Only the word "self".) So I stop talking to my imagined self and begin talking angrily to Brockman. (An imagined Brockman?)

On page 171 Brockman speaks only two words: "Facts smirk." And I say, "Yes, John Brockman. And words suck. And you have sucked me into your world of wastewords." We knew from Beckett that there was nothing to be done. And then you (Yes, You, Brockman) come along and say: "There is nothing to be said." But you keep saying it. Long after I've closed your God Damned book, I hear the choral response that you speak over and over again in *Afterwords*: "I'm still talking." And I see you still smirking. Because you have gotten into my head. But I know that your book is a put-on (Please tell me that it is a put-on so I can forget about it. Admit it, Brockman! You wrote the book with your fingers crossed behind your back.) Because you've made me believe you and I don't want to believe you. Will you please stop telling me that the world is a put-on, that the mind is a put-on.

But of course, I've always known it: We put on our minds every morning at the very same moment that we step into our underwear.

Now do you see the curse of your writing, Brockman. I'm beginning to sound like you.

I'm imitating. I may not be talking, but I'm still writing.

I can't stop. The typewriter has taken over. It's what Brockman has been talking about all along. The *Deus in Machina.* So realize, reader anything you read from here on in is not me writing. It is only the typewriter typing.

Don't you see! Brockman has won. He has got me playing his game.

Game. Game. Game. Game. Game. Game. Game. Game.

Is my mind stuttering? Or my typewriter sticking? Who controls what? I no longer know.

I think the typewriter is thinking. Not the other way around.

Around?

I'll see you around. And my Turkish friend asked, "Around where?" I had no answer because the words had taken over my mind.

Just as the typewriter has taken over my words. And all I can say unto you is &+%@@@@@ + (Help me out of this parenthesis) because "there are only quotation marks left" + $$$$$$$$ and maybe a final period. (Did you ever try for a question mark and blow it? Wind up with only a slash//// (Brockman, get me out of here!)

*   *   *

So do you see what's happening? Do you see what I am trying to say?

Brockman's book scares the shit out of me. It is constant catharsis. I better go back to Judaism where I belong. But then I ask myself: Which is better, Brockman's flux or the constipation of Judaism?

Constipation. Stopped up. Impacted material. Concentrated waste. Blocked shit. Yes, that is what is the *matter* with the world.

O Late John Brockman, godfather of my newborn dead life, tell me what is the speed of shit in an expanding universe?

Listen, Brockman! You are driving me back to Judaism. You can't tell me anything. But the Jew at least has the illusion of a certainty principle. The volcano God who exploded impcratives at Mount Sinai. Doesn't that explain why I have rocks in my head?

So thank you, Brockman, for sending me back to the synagogue. From here on in, it's Me and Buber all the way.

(Is that all? Is that the best you can do? a Me-It relationship?)

I will try for the I-Thou. God how I will try.

"In a world where there are no men, strive to be a man!"
The Talmud

I'm still striving.

Brockman, are you still talking?

I don't hear you talking anymore. I only hear you laughing.

Laughter. Tears. The hysteria of endings.

Brockman, are you there? Over and out.

Brockman, I'm still talking. Are you still listening? Over and out.

Isaac to Control Tower. I can't hear Brockman any more. Shall I try for a landing? Over and out.

Control Tower to Isaac. Ceiling Zero. Go on automatic pilot. Try to come in by instrument.

Isaac to Control Tower. Preparing for crash landing. Here is a last message for Brockman if you can find him: Shma, Brockman! Adonoy Elohenu. Adonoy Echod. Over and out. Signing off.

The Late Rabbi Isaac

THE REALITY OF CONTRADICTION

by Douglas Kelley

In the late sixties, Marshall McLuhan predicted the obsolescence of the book but reconsidered when competing media failed to displace it. It now appears that John Brockman's book *Afterwords* may mark the advent of a new nonlinear print medium which could challenge the book in its traditional form. On the shelf there is nothing to distinguish *Afterwords* from a thousand other soft cover books but upon thumbing through it one is immediately struck by the fact that a large amount of space on each of its three hundred pages has been left unused. Under the old Newtonian view, space was seen as a uniform, continuous container of passive objects which were considered fixed at any instant in time. And until the appearance of *Afterwords* books were containers of uniform, continuous unchanging lines of print fixed in time.

Taking his cue from the quantum physicists who see both fixity at a point in time and continuity as operationally invalid concepts, Brockman has broken up the continuous blocks of print with large intervals of blank space. Using the Heisenberg principle that it is impossible to observe an object without modifying its properties in the process, he transforms the reader into an observer-modifier and gives him the opportunity to change the book by writing his own insights and impressions in the unused space as they occur. The book becomes a a happening, responsive to the reader rather than just a tool for the manufacture of uniform intellects as replaceable parts for the economy. Less obvious technological innovations have changed the character of whole societies. Under this do-it-yourself option the book becomes different for every reader-writer and loses its printing press homogeneity. Every time it is picked up it is subject to change thus losing its Newtonian fixity in time and becoming a new organic print medium. As such, the concept of private authorship becomes obsolete as Brockman shows by incorporating the unmarked quotations of other writers, scientists and poets in the body of his own writing just as the reader will do if he chooses to use the space provided and becomes a reader-writer.

A few years ago we were told that God was dead. Now John Brockman announces that man is dead. What died in the sixties was America's compulsion to substitute the part for the whole. Shortly after the Russians showed us that the moon really did have two sides and was not just another single faced Hollywood prop, Holly-wood died and along with it all our nonwholistic images that de-pended on a fixed, camera side, point of view. The man that is dead is a one-sided man, the John Wayne man, the last cowboy, hero at all times. He was replaced by the two-sided hero-villian, Clint Eastwood. But this image was still only two dimensional. His im-age was still that of the rigid western hero who could only fight or shoot in the direction he was facing. The need was for a hero in touch with his total environment, instantaneously with no concern for unfair attack from the rear. It was supplied by Bruce Lee the first hero of the Chinese martial arts films. Because his art of Kung Fu employs both hands and feet and a fluid dance like body motion it enables him to command instant and wholistic control of the space he occupies against great numbers of attackers. He abolishes the front-rear distinction.

It is necessary to understand that Brockman, Heisenberg and Lee all operate in this oriental kind of space and that the West is rapidly relating to it. For instance everyone felt in the fifties and early sixties that to dismiss bigots as all bad was simplistic but it was not until the seventies that a multidimensional role such as Archie Bunker was acceptable on TV. God is dead because the Beatles have imported a culture whose god is not only one but many and not only male but female. Man is dead because to be all man is to be non-human. It is this recent and total rejection in America of one-sided images that has resulted in the present low regard for politicians and the resulting saleability of the Watergate charges and hearings to the public. It was in the mid-sixties that these changes in public taste pulled the rug out from under the traditional games of government and politics. Brockman explores how it is that the best and the brightest could have been so wrong and he finds that a large part of the answer is that they had been "nouned."

In the use of nouns as labels for perceptions we have mistaken the labels for reality in the sense that we have created the idea of an "object" which is supposed to be the counterpart in reality of the noun. Physics has never found an object, only force fields.

The result of this objectification of reality is that the total interrelatedness of reality is lost as attention is focused on separate "objects." Man becomes an object trapped on a second object which he nouns earth and which he sees as dragging him in circles through an alien universe. God became nouned into a separate being "out there," the meaning of Christ's words "God is in you" having been lost for four hundred years until rediscovered by Tim Leary and Richard Alpert. The universe had become a billiard ball affair moving, we were told, in mathematically precise orbits. How did it get there? Who made it? Why God, of course, The Big Clock Maker. These are the images of God and man that have died.

When reality is objectified so is rationality and it is supposed that truth is found by being "objective". But to be objective is to be an object, dead, only partially in touch. Blacks are generally speaking not objective and it is the resulting high degree of involvement which they term "soul." The current debate on black IQ's is nothing more than an attempt on Jensen's and Herrenstein's parts, albeit unconscious, to resurrect man the rational animal in whose image they have modeled themselves and who as Brockman observes is dead. They are not yet ready to accept that theirs is merely the old Newtonian brand of rationality which as the counter culture tried to indicate must now share the stage with wholistic rationality.

The reader will initially be put off by the many contradictory statements in *Afterwords*. The fear of contradictions is among the most costly biases of the Western world. A feature of the new rationality is that it can make sense of contradictions. This has been done by British mathematician G. Spencer Brown who has shown that a whole class of contradictions in the field of logic are the direct result of our refusal to leave anything unnamed, unlabelled, unnouned. He has demonstrated mathematically that contradictions arise when we try to confine statements of logic to the two dimensional plane. He has given us a precise formulation of this new logic, it is the logic of Brockman, Heisenberg and Bruce Lee. Thus in reading *Afterwords* it is essential to seek out the contradictions rather than avoid them. They tell us where language breaks down as a representation of reality and thus where the hangups are. On the apparently plane surface of the earth it is appropriate to use the either-or logic of the plane and say "it is either night or day." But to use an example from *Afterwords*, when we view the earth from outer space it is no longer a plane but three dimensional, a sphere and here we must switch to the both-and logic of higher dimensions and say "it is both night and day" as the photographs from Apollo clearly illustrate. The big bang-steady state debate as to the origin of the universe is nothing more than this inappropriate use of the either-or dichotomy. The universe is both big bang and steady state. From higher levels of consciousness this becomes a matter of direct perception just as does the fact that it is both night and day when the earth is viewed from higher levels of altitude. The Hindu writings contain rather detailed accounts of the combination big bang-steady state nature of the universe which Western cosmologists are only beginning to duplicate through the jnana yoga of mathematics. It is interesting to note here that although G. Spencer Brown was unaware of the Hindu sources at the time of his work, he now agrees that the steps in the mathematical development of his logic parallel very closely the Hindu account of the origin of the universe.

The reader must be open to perceptions in the form of immediate insights as in poetry. At the creative level science becomes art. To promote this process Brockman avoids explanations in *Afterwords*. The latin roots of the word explain mean to lay out in a plane and we have seen that this is just the process of decreation that has trapped Western thinking since Aristotle.

RE: *AFTERWORDS*

by Richard Kostelanetz

John Brockman's three books are not as incomprehensible as they might initially seem; indeed they are at base quite simple.

The first takes information theory – the mathematical theory of communications – as a model for regarding all human experience.

The second is a print portrait of Heisenberg's theory of indeterminacy.

The third investigates the limits of words as tools for understanding.

What distinguishes this trilogy is not their informing hypotheses, which are familiar to various degrees, but the author's unfettered exploration of their implications.

I also admire enormously their style and structure, as well as their remarkable capacity to implant themselves in the reader's mind.

"UREA: I FOUND IT!"

by Paul A. Lee

Historical Perspective

The crucial date is 1828, when a German chemist, named Wohler, synthesized, ostensibly through artificial means, or chemically contrived simulants, an organic substance, urea, a product of the kidneys. In the standard texts of the history of science, it is almost uniformly regarded as a decisive moment - when *Physicalism,* or the forces marshalled by Newton, defeated *Vitalism,* or the forces marshalled by Goethe.[1] It was some defeat, in the sense that Goethe's forces represented a traditional leading back to Homer, the "Epic tradition of the perfect tense of essential man", a tradition which had determined, up to this moment, the basic meaning of man's self-interpretation, what usually goes by the name of the Humanities, in quest of *sapientia,* or wisdom. Newtonian *scientia,* the Royal Society, the Experimental Laboratory, Industry, and Technology - these were the allied forces whose victory was assured for nearly a century and a half, if one takes as a symbolic date the significance of Professor Wohler's efforts - even though he still used a modicum of organic elements in his synthesis. If it wasn't exactly a *clean* sweep - they still sang Christmas Carols to the old professor while working in the laboratory on Christmas Eve - all the same, *scientia,* in the Indian arm-wrestling of the age, pressed its opponent all the way down. *Sapientia* went underground.

A few years later, to bear witness to the defeat dealt to the Humanities, when *Wissenschaft* lost its *Geistes,* when the Quarrel between the Ancients and the Moderns was decided in favor of the Moderns and the re-organization of *what counts for knowledge* was decided in favor of the Physicalists, a movement of protest was initiated to point out some of the disastrous consequences eventually to appear. It was a prophetic movement of thought designed to protest against the distorted forms of dehumanization, alienation, and estrangement, resulting from the reduction of the organic to the inorganic, the natural to the non-natural, the genuine to the simulated, the authentic to the *ersatz,* i.e., a protest against the emergence of Technical Society - the world above the given world of nature - (Wohler's artificial synthesis is basic to the development of the *plastics* industry, as in poly-*ure*-thane). *Existentialism* had its historic inception in the Berlin lectures of the great *Naturphilosophe* - Schelling - in 1841-42, with Jacob Burckhardt, Engels, Bakunin, and Søren Kierkegaard sitting in the classroom. *Existentialism, then, is to be seen as chief mourner for defeated Vitalism,* playing its part as an historic protest against the elimination and destruction of man's organic essence. (After all, didn't J.J. Rodale have to re-introduce the word "organic" into the English language after Wohler's inorganic synthesis displaced the word.) The mopping-up operation as a follow-through of the Physicalist victory was to eliminate metaphysics and consciousness, as well. This was accomplished in two phases: (1) by the philosophical alignment known as *Logical Positivism,* a school of thought centered in the Viennese Circle around Professor Rudolf Carnap. In an effort to consolidate the gains of modern science, Carnap envisaged a universal mathematic, or unified scientific language, or system of signs, after the vision of a universal logic of Leibniz, uniting the international community of scholars deserving the name of scientist. One of the ironies of the history of Carnap's school was the undoing of his Positivist pretensions by his own student, Kurt Godel, whose Incompleteness Theorems, and justly celebrated *Godel's Proof,* refuted Carnap's ambitions (although they ran their course, nevertheless), by demonstrating that a universal system of logic was incapable of specifying its own internal consistency, which only *another* system could specify. (2) Reductive behaviourism and its angry cats finally came up with the absurd pretensions of B.(eyond) F.(reedom) (and Dignity) Skinner - there are more ways than one to skin a cat - accompanied by the absolute triumph of experimental chemistry over consciousness in the discovery of lycergic acid diethylamide, by the Sandoz chemist, Hoffman, which confirmed the elimination of metaphysics in the psychedelic *destruction* of consciousness. This brings us, finally, to the *Afterwords* of the late John Brockman and the first sentence in the book from which all else follows: "Man is dead."

From the Positivist and Behaviourist Elimination of Metaphysics to the Psychedelic Destruction of Consciousness

John Brockman is fond of quoting Ludwig Wittgenstein and well he might be. Wittgenstein is the exemplar of the age of the destruction of consciousness. In the trenches of World War I, while everyone else called upon their "Lieber Gott" (as in *Waiting for Godot* - no answer), with his *Tractatus* in his knapsack, Wittgenstein suffered the close-out sale of the *Ansverkauf der Werte,* when the bargain counter of cultural values were sold out altogether. Put simply, as only Wittgenstein could put it, in behalf of all of us, whether in the trenches, or out of the trenches, I don't know, God knows, Wittgenstein lost his sense of human decency. Henceforth, as though to symbolize the loss, he never again wore a tie, to indicate that he could not take his place in the company of decent men. The removal of "Wittgenstein's tie" is the metaphor, the existential *ikon,* of the world come of age, the world without value, the disinherited mind, the mind burdened by the *anxiety of meaninglessness and emptiness,* as Paul Tillich put it in his unintentional portrait of Wittgenstein as 20th century *urmensch* - he who has the courage to take *this* anxiety upon himself, has the courage to be. In this sense, "man is dead" can become an affirmation, a peculiar twist Brockman has learned some of the knots for. It is the condition of the "sacred void." After the destruction of conscious-ness, the primary question is its reconstitution, which the coming decade will decide. We have just ten years before 1984. Brockman's book is both epitaph and portent.

From Wittgenstein's Tie to Godel's Proof, or, To Tie the Knot Again

When you lose your sense of human decency (and to what extent this is to be seen as 1) a departure from the bourgeois class of con-ventions; 2) an exodus from institutional bondage; 3) as a forfeiture of one's humanity - we leave for future discussion); when you end up in a Norwegian hut reading Kierkegaard's *Edifying Discourses,* in an effort to restore what is missing *(aber etwas fehlt);* when you see through all language as so many mind-games, and you waver over the question - must we *mean* what we say?; when you could just as well leave the upper part of the pages blank as the lower part, and instead provide footnotes for a text left to the reader to supply; when any-one's meaning is anyone's nonsense because you come after the psychedelic destruction of consciousness and before its authentic and normative reconstitution; when you are conquered by the vertigo of existence, in the Pascalian sense of why *here,* rather than *there,* why *now* rather than *then;* when the terror of history engulfs the sense of place; when philosophy becomes the disease of which it should be the cure; when any simulation run counts as much as the real thing; when "reality," rather than grasping itself in thought, is *just* another word . . . (whatever you think of the problem "Is existence a predi-cate?", do you ever wake up in the middle of the night and still feel the ultimate concern for imperishable bliss?) . . . even so, my friends, and that includes John Brockman, at this very moment, Kurt Godel, the greatest living mathematical logician is working on a proof for the existence of God, and even though Professor Godel quite rightly wonders about what his theo-*logy* has to do with consciousness, perhaps in the old sense of what does Athens have to do with Jerusalem, what does the god of the logicians have to do with the God of Abraham, Isaac, and Jacob; and even though we don't know whether or not anyone would take off their shoes before the burning bush of proof; still, as Octavio Paz said, "It will change everything."

Counting Your Chickens Before They Hatch

When, for the poet, existence becomes a predicate again; when, for the physicist, Godel's new proof for the existence of God provides the ground and abyss for Einstein's unified field theory; when, for the philosopher, thought, even the thought of the logician (who might not want to have anything to do with it) becomes prayer, and the poet and the logician transcend themselves (as in the dying words of Hermann Broch's Virgil) and reduplicated existence is unduplicated in communion, then even our enemies are vindicated, and "we are all one two three four ever" (Gerd Stern) in that mystical "coincidence of opposites" the Bishop of Cues, Nicholas, known as Cusanus, foresaw in the Middle Ages. The mystical limits of contemporary reality are best seen today in Huey P. Newton's vision of "intercommunalism," as in the highest vision of the Apostle Paul, where the mystical limits are understood in words no one may dare utter, when with sighs too deep for words, we perceive that God will be all in all.

Notes

(1) We denominate Newton and Goethe as the exemplary figures in the Physicalist/Vitalist struggle, partly because of Goethe's efforts to refute Newton's optics, in his theory of color, and partly because of the continuation of Goethe's scientific work by Rudolf Steiner, the founder of anthroposophy. Steiner is a test case in the almost ruthless elimination of vitalism from higher education and the re-organization of knowledge culminating in the lumping of spiritualism, metaphysics and mysticism in one rejected package. Steiner was the editor of Goethe's scientific writings in the Goethe archive at Weimar. The Newton-Goethe split and the conflict between Physicalism and Vitalism is the reference point for the "Two Cultures" controversy of C.P. Snow, and *The Structure of Scientific Revolutions,* by Thomas Kuhn. With-

out this reference point, Snow is superficial and Kuhn is formalistic; with it, their analyses begin to make sense. Two studies are helpful: Ernst Cassirer, *The Problem of Knowledge,* and John Merz, *History of Scientific Thought in the 19th Century.*

(2) cf. "The Ballad of Cock Robin."

> "Who killed Cock Robin? *(Vitalism)*
> I said the sparrow *(Physicalism)*
> with my bow and arrow. *(Artificial Synthesis of Urea)*
> Who will be the chief mourner?
> I said the Dove *(Existentialism)*
> because of my love."

Not until 1963, with the publication of Rachel Carson's *Silent Spring,* who made the late Cock Robin a popular cause called "ecology" did the forces of *neo*-vitalism gather strength until the national seizure of conscience on Earth Day, April 22, 1970, which we take to be the formal ending of the Existentialist period and the re-enjoining of the debate broken off in the late 19th Century. There were spokesmen for the vitalist cause - Bergson and Albert Schweitzer. "Reverence for life" becomes something more than a slogan for satisfying vicarious spiritual longings on the part of middle-class professionals to hang on their office walls and more of the order of existential protest as we describe it. Schweitzer could be seen then as *the* chief mourner personified in his exodus from Western civilization and its institutional bondage to the Physicalist oath to darkest Africa where Black *Soul* sustained Vitalist integrity.

AN AMERICAN JNANA YOGA

by John C. Lilly

My debt to John Brockman is great: he taught me the essential non-existence of the screen of words. By defining, with words, the non-existence of definitions, the experience without words becomes the highest value in the hierarchy. The injunctive use of words (as in a cookbook) pointing to experience yet to be had is the only worthwhile residuum of "the filmiest of screens separating ordinary reality from the non-ordinary realities" inside one's own inner spaces. To paraphrase litero-clastic word-destroyer friend J.B., all statements (including this one) *about* reality are false; all statements (including this one) *from* reality are true; reality speaks only through our experience of it.

Afterwords is a compilation of ideas collected, computed, re-screened, re-ordered, re-created in the biocomputer of John Brockman. Despite his argument that the screen of words ("Man") is dead, he manipulates the screen in a unique living fishnet which captures important ideas in an American jnana yoga. There are flashes of cosmic humor, dispassionate critiques, important operations of the mind, and a super head trip.

POST-LIFE FELICITATIONS

by John McHale & Magda Cordell

Wishing 33^3 years to
the Late(r) Brock Johnman:
in-visible, in-effable, in-eluctable
polymathman.
Specterman of the Brocken.
Doppelgangerman of the 'Stein.
Scribeman: Spiderman: Hu-man.
Long-life, Hi-life, Pre and
Post-life Felicitations.

ON JOHN BROCKMAN

by Richard Morris

1.

I have nothing to say and I am saying it.
- John Cage

2.

Brockman's *Afterwords* is ("like Gaul," I am tempted to say) divided
into three parts. In the first, he does away with man. In the second,
he attempts, somewhat less successfully, to abolish the universe. In
the third, he shows us what we always knew: that the world is
meaningless.

3.

Man is dead, Brockman tells us. "Man" is an abstraction, a model
that is no longer useful. Neither are such concepts as "consciousness,"
"feelings," "emotions," "mind," "ego," "spirit," "soul," "pain."
All experience can be accounted for in terms of neural operations.
Nothing else is happening. The brain has an input, and it produces
an output. There is no "thought". Man is dead.

4.

At first, Brockman seems to be replacing one set of abstractions with
another. But then he stops to tell us, "The author doesn't believe a
word of what is set forth and is not interested in formulation of new
dogma." Man is dead. The model of the brain as an input-output
mechanism is no more real than the concept "man".

5.

"Man" is a model that no longer works. But don't replace it with a new model. Experience is not to be interpreted this way; experience simply *is*.

6.

Brockman is not explaining anything here. There is nothing to be explained. He is making an injunction: do not make models. "Reality" is not in any model; it simply is.

7.

If there are no questions, there are no answers.
                                                    - John Cage

8.

Sometimes Brockman's statements are obscure or meaningless. "The operation of the brain is a nonlinear process." What does "nonlinear" mean in this context? Brockman speaks of "operant patterns on the neural level." What is "operant" here? He states Godel's proof in an odd way: "For any formal system capable of producing arithmetic there is a truism proving the system which cannot be proven within the system." Would someone not already familiar with the proof understand this? Brockman then goes on to replace "system" by "consciousness," and apply the proof to man. This is nonsense.

9.

But if one is saying there are no explanations, must his statements always make sense? Isn't it enough that they are suggestive?

10.

Brockman has replaced "man" with neural patterns in the brain.

Man and all the abstractions associated with the existence of "man" are dead. But don't believe any of this, he warns, we can no longer use models (sets of abstractions). So much for Part I.

11.

Part II is less successful. Universe does not exist either, Brockman says. There is only the mathematical description. The mathematical description *is* the thing. The verbal models we make do not mean anything; they are unjustified extrapolations.

12.

Therefore, do not use the "rotted names": mind, space, time, people, place, life, death, world.

13.

Truth is a matter of convenience, Brockman claims. Nothing makes any difference. There is nothing left to say. We cannot know more than we know. Facts smirk. Our knowledge has led us one place: nowhere; our knowledge has proven one thing: nothing.

14.

None of this is entirely satisfying. For one thing, the strategy of reducing the universe to mathematical description is not as convincing as the strategy of reducing man to neural impulses. The trouble is that any mathematical description is just another language with its own "rotted names." It is also a model.

15.

I am objecting to one of Brockman's premises. He would say, there are no premises.

16.

But the rest of Part II is no more convincing. Like Wittgenstein, Brockman wants to climb his ladder, and then throw the ladder away. But if one does not construct the ladder well enough, he will will not get to a place where he can dispense with it.

17.

One cannot disagree with Brockman. To do so, one would have to use the abstractions that Brockman will not admit into the argument. But one can refuse to be enlightened after being shown Brockman's ways of looking.

18.

The trouble is that when one finishes reading Part II, he finds that, in spite of all Brockman's efforts, the universe persists.

19.

The world is unintelligble, Brockman says in Part III. Something we've always known. But it takes someone like Brockman to point it out. The world does not mean anything. It is neither significant or absurd. It *is*.

20.

Get rid of the comfort words, he tells us. All concepts are waste. Comfort words: magic, myth, religion, art, ideology, science, literature. Meaning and necessity are preserved only in the linguistic practices which embody them.

21.

The world is unintelligble. We've always known that. But we weren't willing to admit it. (Now it is "I" who am speaking; I am no longer paraphrasing "Brockman".) It has been the business of Western civilization to impose an order on chaos, ever since the Greeks began making the world conform to the grammar of their language. Thus the scientist imposes order upon a chaotic universe, while the artist imposes order upon unintelligble experience.

22.

The constructs are breaking down. At one time we could say "Life imitates Art." It was the business of the artist to make the models by which we interpreted "human experience." But we no longer have single accepted artistic traditions or agreed-upon models. We are approaching the point where experience simply *is*.

23.

One could go on talking about this fragmentation that is so characteristic of the modern experience; the models are breaking down everywhere. Even in physics. When classical physics began to disintegrate, we were able to replace it with quantum mechanics and with relativity. But now the mathematical model provided by quantum mechanics is beginning to break down also, and we can no longer be certain that we will find a new model to replace it.

24.

At this point Brockman would add, "Don't believe it. Don't believe anything I say. There is nothing to say, nothing to think about."

25.

What Brockman writes is not philosophy. He is no more a philospher than John Cage is a composer. He's not even a poet. Most poets, like most physicists, are still trying to put order into the world.

26.

How long will they be able to continue the attempt?

27.

The world is unintelligble.

28.

Here we are. Let us say Yes to our presence together in Chaos.
                                        -John Cage

29.

I was almost tempted to end this piece with that quotation. It seems to have the proper note of finality; it implies that Brockman, like a few artists such as Cage, are concerned with bringing us into contact with the Chaos that is reality.

30.

But Brockman (and probably Cage also) would deny that there is such a thing as "chaos." Or "finality," or "reality," for that matter.

31.

Don't believe any of this.
                - John Brockman

I've seen nothing.
                - John Cage (quoting Satie)

WORDS FROM "FACT'S RAZOR"

by Michael Perkins

I first came across the work of John Brockman because I was attracted to the title, *By The Late John Brockman,* and to the severe brown wrappers which cover both of his hardcover books (now republished in paperback as Part I and Part II of *Afterwords,* along with new work as Part III). The first sentence of *By The Late John Brockman* is the statement: "Man is dead." I couldn't allow such a sweeping statement to pass: who was this Brockman, 1941-1969? Finally I had to read his books, if for no other reason than to test his presumptuousness. After reading his work I almost regret my curiosity; it has pulled me, kicking and screaming, into a new way of viewing my dead world. No one likes to be bothered that mightily by a contemporary. Nevertheless, here I am with a newly cleared head - as after a major illness - and a new set of names for everything. But where to begin to discuss what Brockman says cannot be discussed? *Everything is as it seems/There are no questions to be answered after all/Curiosity is the other side of silence/Each sign means what it says/ How it strikes you, not what is meant/Symbols are the coins we clank when we have nothing to say/Literature is a cork-lined room to retire to/Its strictures are the diaries of old maids/Disappear into the clock face/Vanish into the present/Saying makes it so/Everything is as it seems.*

Like many writers I've always had what can only be termed a blind instinct for the given, and a distrust of symbols. Like a child, the factuality, or in Brockman's words, the "is-ness" of something has always seemed more interesting than the meanings it accrues. Just as interesting are the *names* we give to experience. Brockman challenges me to give a name to him, to his work, and I suppose that is the real function of any review: to name what the writer is doing, however ignorantly; to make a scratch on the glass distinct enough to interest others.

To begin with, many of Brockman's words are not his own. He is dictated to, and transcribes what he received, like a child of his age hearing the words of "masters" through a receiver which by its very technology transforms past wisdom into mathematical codes we are just beginning to learn how to read. Artaud, Niels Bohr, John Cage, Marshall McLuhan, Don Juan, Rene Dubos, Loren Eiseley, Buckminster Fuller, Jung, Whitehead, Norbert Wiener, Einstein, William Empson, Heisenberg, Wittgenstein, Wallace Stevens, Paul Valery, Robbe-Grillet: these are the voices of John Brockman. Brockman often seems like a crystal set on another planet, vaguely resembling ours, receiving isolated and warped messages long after its human operators are dead. Which means simply that Brockman is barely able to keep pace with the exploding present, and rather than being difficult to comprehend, "terrifying," or "futuristic gibberish," as other reviewers have averred, what he is saying seems obvious, once some basic propositions are understood.

Part I of *Afterwords,* put as "rationally" as possible, and thus falsified, is an attempt to demonstrate the singular importance of the brain as sole receiver of direct, immediate experience. "Consciousness, feelings, emotions, mind, ego, spirit, soul, pain, etc., words resulting from centuries of belief, and no longer useful.... Man is an abstraction. Human abstractions are based on the past, not on operant considerations of what is happening . . ." Brockman's concern is with what is happening *right now.* Consider the possibilities of technology, and you will begin to grasp his meaning. "The activity of which man could never be aware, the direct experience of the brain. Man is dead. Men never existed at all. Our awareness as experience is past experience. Dreaming . . . All that is real can be found in the operations of the brain . . . Causality and sequence are myths. Sequence is simultaneity!" The "meaning" of the title (*By The Late John Brockman*) is simply that Brockman cannot exist in a book printed even five minutes ago.

Part II goes beyond the simple negative statement of Part I that nothing exists beyond what the brain immediately is bombarded with, to negate all that we have previously assumed: history, philosophy, the generalizations of previous epochs. The one shows us what is actually going on, and the other clears the attic of all the scrapbooks of the past. "We must not assume the existence of any entity until we are compelled to do so." Brockman is talking about the negation of history, of the weight of assumption. "Any absolute statement relating to properties of the world around us must be considered as an unjustified extrapolation. Only a description based on observations and relative to the process of observation can be valid . . . Facts smirk."

Part II is the large end of the telescope considering the three books he has written. In it he is most expansive in his discussion of names and meaning. I consider it his most accessible and exciting work. He is too far ahead of McLuhan to be compared with him, but I think that in due time his work will find an audience of similar dimensions. But perhaps a paragraph like the following might frighten the book-oriented: "Words do not signify anything but their own reality. Words do not create the universe out of nothing but out of all. All possibilities exist in any: the whole story from Genesis to Apocalypse in any event; in any metamorphoses."
And after he has said that, he adds: "Don't believe it. Don't believe anything I say. There's nothing to say. I have nothing to say. There's nothing to think about." Or: thinking makes it so.
Part III simply negates a wider area than the previous two works.

Only in the course of thinking - immediately as I write - about Brockman's work has a "name" for him as a writer of these books occurred to me. He is fact's razor, cutting away everything - *everything* - knowledge, meaning, emotion, that we have let grow around us to keep out the cold of nothingness. If he follows his own lines, there is nothing left for him to say, but like Beckett, I suppose he will go on writing. Ideally, as in Zen, his ideas would be demonstrated, but unspoken. It won't be difficult for future critics to find his weak spots - the attention-getting anger, the simplistic generalizations which sometimes dominate a page - but I doubt that anyone who reads him with understanding will be able to escape his thinking.

VARIATIONS ON A THEME BY BROCKMAN

by R.S. Picciotto

Man is dead.

John Brockman is dead.

I am dead.

In fact, there is no reason to believe that we ever existed.

Man, Brockman, myself, abstractions all three, reflections of the thing itself. Of what? Whereof one knows not, thereof one must remain silent.

The present is all there is, over before the abstraction "this is the present" shapes itself.

The illusion of the present is all there is, loaded with illusions of illusions, each fitting within the other like dolls made by Slavic peasants:

illusions of writing "Variations on a Theme by Brockman";

illusions of having read a book called *Afterwords;*

illusions that each statement in the book touched on others to shape a picture, as the chips of stone in a Roman mosaic together yield a maid with a pitcher on her shoulder;

illusions that the chips of stone yield not only the maid, but the hand of the arranger and the arranger himself;

illusions that the words of *Afterwords* yield not only the thoughts, but the mind of the thinker and the thinker himself -

since they too are an illusion, unpurged by reality;

illusions that the words of *Afterwords* make Brockman as their maker, invent him as their inventor,

as the illusion of man might invent god as its inventor;

illusions that the words of *Afterwords* do not belong to Brockman nor Brockman to them,

but are all one,

alone,

Brockman,

creator of statements that self-destruct, of time that self-destructs, of self that self-destructs,

so that all that is left are the "Variations on a Theme by Brockman,"

making me as their maker.

FISSURES IN MEANING

by Bern Porter

Techniques for changing direction, quantity, dimension; for impinging, bombarding, scattering; for diffusing, projecting, condensing; for counting, sorting, identifying; for recording, remembering, retrieving are exemplary of the manifold techniques making possible ultra technological achievements: nuclear fission, plasma containment, space flight. With every advance of the basic formulas in all the branches of the sciences the creators approach the gaping abyss; the thin division separating them from total annihilation on one side and the world's greatest, most permanent culture on the other.

In the dividing plane space resides undisturbed the highest of all accomplishments, the word.

And between the words, lies the ultimate enigma, meaning.

Wherein and whereby must the membrane separating us from the last imponderable be pushed back, be pierced; be surmounted, passed over, circumvented, made permanently open? By what password, what magic key, what procedure?

Sadly the methodologies are unavailable. ("Nobody knows, and you can't find out," says Brockman in the very last line of his *Afterwords*.)

Such admonishments as "except ye become as little children," "resort all my brethren to blind faith," "accept the truth and it will set you free" recede into the background as mere earwash while the cohorts of science pound impenetrable walls. "When I push an indentation here," complains Einstein, "a bulge appears over there."

The Brockman route holds promise.

I first encountered it as wall paper, as a decorative motif, a vertical sheathing blanket, pages overlapped like shingles to keep the cold out, the heat in. Carefully printed sheets of book paper, complete pages rent from their binding (80% of the first editions of *By The Late John Brockman,* 1969 and *37,* 1970 were remaindered) contained on their collective surfaces a potential blueprint for the way out, over and into.

Interestingly, close examination of their revised form in the single, September 7, 1973 publication shows a complete synthesis involving 277 references, 56 authors, 6 especially selected books, the whole equating 27,000,000 words spanning 200 years of living and thought. This third level of interpretation could only be made possible by the 50,000,000 borrowed words at the supporting second stage, while the first generation, the beginning of it all, would equate to 80,000,000 words and 2000 years.

And none of it yet subjected to the fullest, or even the remotest kinds of scientific research cited in our opening paragraph for say the development of a transistor.

Under such a mountainous array, between which words, even what words, lies meaning? Or are they all worthless? 157,000,000 of them?

Brockman affirms they are.

And in that event, it's the fissures, the spaces between words, the blank spots between meanings that matter.

Are not we physicists still bombarding the spaces between the subdivisions of identifiable matter with gigantic electron accelerators? Hoping to get through?

Brockman, alone on the other side, in that quiet there, quiet because he is the only one there, can hope the rest of us may yet make it.

AFTERWORDS **CAN**

by Edwin Schlossberg

AFTERWORDS

        comes the possibility of considering complex
                conversations
        comes the option of undifferentiated description
        comes the ability to conceive of space and time and
                thinking without hesitation
        comes the ubiquity of signals
        comes the organizing of a new communications
                methodology
        comes the opportunity for another silence
        comes the level of speculation necessary
        comes the reinvigoration of themselves themselves
        comes the kind of emptiness needed
        comes the height of letters

        is filled with new words
        is crowded with options
        is leveled by teleology
        is the concern for a yet unformulated noise
        is deemed the arena for sustained searching
        is the focus of the those before
        is the absence of pedigree
        is the engaged opinions of non-uniform congruence
        is the width of complementary behavior
        is the lack of words

        has no answer
        has no formula
        has no contract
        has no center

has no edge
has no possibilities
has no future
has little past
has no concern
has some time
has little hypothesis worth remembering in words
has deemed itself thoughtless

can evade criticism
can deny oversight
can relent pessimism
can undue scholastic tautology
can revoke silence
can unsettle belief
can hide neurosis
can guage perspective
can underline absence
can

SOUNDS

by Alan Sondheim

I am writing this on the way from London to Newcastle-on-Tyne.
The train has an automatic voice system, and somehow the signals
have gotten mixed up. Stops are announced that are non-existent,
and we pull up at anonymous stations. The *London Times* for the
day carries such headlines as "Lights go out as emergency powers
bite," "Three weeks needed to start petrol rationing," "Floodlights
off," "Fuel cut order," "Ambulance ban," and "Halt London' call."
The last reads, in full: "A combined pay strike to halt London's
entire public transport system - Tube trains, buses, and commuter
trains - was urged yesterday by the London district council of the
Associated Society of Locomotive Engineers and Firemen. Details,
page 2." All of these items refer to the Capital itself. The paper
is a blur of other items - the Mideast crisis, Watergate, etc. etc.
All of this in the form of cries, unsteady words, anonymous
journalism.

John Brockman's work is the newspaper of consciousness. It is
frankly, enormously important on a number of different levels. I
shall try to make some of these clear in this article.

Just as "public" statements become anonymous grist for news-
papers, various isolated ideas become the core of Brockman's work.
These ideas are often lifted bodily from other writers; there is a
complete and necessary negation of the concept of ownership. The
information of the world is sifted, and a certain essence shaped by
Brockman; the result is a book, Brockman's own.

The essence is verbal, neural, occasionally logical. The world is
words, the world does not exist. We are on a plane of neural move-
ments and moments. Only occasionally does something else come
through, something in fact reminiscent of Wittgenstein's pronounce-
ments at the end of his *Tractatus*. Towards the end of the third

section, Brockman writes: "I can't think of one anymore. This or that: I can't differentiate anymore. I don't believe it: I can't think, I must not try to think, simply utter. Saying makes it so. This, this and that: I shall have to banish them in the end, the beings, shapes sounds, and lights which with my haste to speak have encumbered this place." The words are Brockman's and Beckett's, and, of course, they are ours.

Words cover the contemporary world. More than that, they are generally systematized. The Americans pride themselves on their logic. We all know that this has resulted in an abstract vocabulary, containing words such as "defoliation" which are applied, but hardly applicable, to human problems. Now a system is generally governed by clear-cut rules; it contains elements, and transformations between them. Certain things are defined as elements, and certain things are defined as not-elements. The logic generally employed is classical, two-valued. Further, time may enter the notion of a system; we can create a "time-slice" and specify its state at any particular instant.

All well and good - until such thinking is applied to the "real world." A great deal of the present difficulty in London is due to an elimination of overtime work by the miners. This is going to create a serious fuel shortage, compounded by the Middle East oil situation. The shortage may result in a complete London blackout . On the other hand, the miners are among the poorest paid workers in Britain, doing one of the most difficult jobs. An unheard-of 500 miners are leaving the pits each week, for good. And there are only a quarter of a million of them in Britain. I could go on and on - the point is that any sort of "system" is going to break down here. The rules are changing constantly, there is no "true" or "false", no "right" or "wrong". Further, and perhaps most important, we cannot create a "time-slice" of "facts" for any given moment. Both personal and public communications channels are already overloaded, the situation is in flux, etc.

Here, for this writer, is the importance of Brockman's work. It negates systems, takes a tough stand: "The world is made up, not made. The world is created, and created things can no longer be considered as intermediaries leading to an infinity of other things. They are dead: they are their own fictions, begin and end in themselves, live and die in themselves. Created things are dead. The life you live is a lie. The world you inhabit is a lie. There is no need for fiction in the world: the world is the only fiction."

The book conforms to its own position: It moves in various directions, seemingly at once, hammering home things that are occasionally given the status of slogan: "Man is dead." "No man's land." "Our knowledge has proven one thing: nothing." "Disposable world." "Reject world." "Nobody knows, and you can't find out." (Take this last in relation to *any* news story.) The pages can be read in any order, no, that's not true, only some of them can. The cross-linkages are there, and mysterious.

At times the prose appears to be without any author altogether; even when he appears, he is a shadow. His negations move beyond philosophy; they attack the notion of communication itself: "No man is my friend. I have no interest in the human condition. No interest in you, your ideas, your words. No interest in your opinions. . .Don't believe it. Don't believe anything I say. There's nothing to say. I have nothing to say. There's nothing to think about." The facileness of the writing hides its complexity. The logical and semantic structure, for example, of "Don't believe anything I say. There's nothing to say." is extraordinarily complex. It is similar to the old paradox contained in such statements as "All Cretans are liars. I am a Cretan." But, more than that - if the latter sentence is true ("There's nothing to say."), then the former is meaningless. . .(Creating an extended metaphor, we could write "Brockman is a miner of words, refusing to work overtime." As such, his activity mirrors our world; the distortions of language above contain as much "meaning" as the current situation in Britain. But, just as the current situation vitally affects and challenges the "average" Londoner, so does Brockman's work attack intellectualizations. By observing them, by refusing to participate in them, Brockman reveals their ambiguity, their instability.)

To conclude - the book bothers me. The first section is one of the strongest challenges to existentialist and phenomenological attitudes that I have ever read. It veers between pain and pronouncement - the author's and our own. We are in this together. We are involved in a strange sort of surrender, for we are using the same forms of communication that are being nihilated. I'm not even sure who "we" refers to here, nor, at least according to "Brockman," who "I" am. Or, in "fact" "who" "I" "am". It has to be let, at that, and isn't as simple as it sounds.

ABOUT BROCKMAN'S *AFTERWORDS*

by Gerd Stern

Back in '68 JB and I
He wheeling a short in his life yellow Jaguar
I flying executive
met at the Boat Slip motel in P-town
to write a book of ideas
on multi inter arts media
For several days we wandered, rapped, caucussed
and wrote hardly a word down
By the weekend my young lady friend arrived
and in our room adjacent to his
we made several days of noisy love
pausing only to eat with JB
and then get back into each other's skins
He, distracted by our noise, wrote
and when she left read me the first bits
by the late John Brockman

                    *

By the time that book arrived
I had given up matching for parity:
the late writer with the friend persona
or the then popular death of G-D
with his newly referenced death of M-N

                    *

The book, and his second *37*
embarrassed old friends and relatives
Instead of producing compliments and table talk
they provoked Cageish silences and accusations of fraud
Denying in writing existence, belief and value

by quotation, citation, interpretation, intermodulation
he wasn't about to voice an in person defence of that evidence
Now in the three-in-one *Afterwords*
Brockman makes plainer by simple weight
of statement, restatement and redundant statement
his technological consciousness
a matrixed vision
of NOW/IS happenstance

*

From Wiener to Heisenberg, Stein to Stevens
others'words are embedded and absorbed
in the terse, ideational paragraphics,
without quotes simply referenced in the back of the book
They come first, last or inbetween Brockman's thoughts
as one's own mind process ingests and digests observation
producing a set for insight, independent of original context
a risky, valuable new type of literary conglomerate

*

The bottom half of the book
could be cut off without losing a Brockman word
Some of the single-paged thoughts occupy only a line
Such a blankness of paper disturbs
the waste not and the I want more
but by design isolates each statement
in white space; creating the tabula rasa
necessary for next and etcetera
the possibilities of back and forth and through

*

Each page as a scan
is a real-time event
broadcasting an imaged signal
blocking the readers' I-noise generator

This word process is a state-of-the-art phenomenon
found-object extrapolation and integration
like information theory, nuclear physics, micro-biology
music and video synthesis - and depends on those ideas of order

peculiar to this decade and the future

As such this process is not culpable of the old *understanding*
Scan it like a tube - get a fix on it in that perspective
perceive it going out of focus and out of sight.

EPILOGUE TO *AFTERWORDS*

by Heinz Von Foerster

Afterwords to John Brockman's *Afterwords* should best be written by John Brockman. In fact, he wrote it. It is *Afterwords*. They are put into 292 propositions to be found on pages paginated correspondingly. He who holds paginated blank pages against my counting them as propositions still travels in the semantic universe of forewords. Forewords are propositions which are designed to do some other words: those which follow. Afterwords undo themselves, including their precursors. Post-Wittgensteinean epistomologists first wrestled with, and are now slowly beginning to understand, the last proposition (No. 7) of Wittgenstein's *Tractatus Logico Philosophicus:* "Of which we cannot speak we have to remain silent". Brockman understands. Afterwords silence themselves. His last proposition (No. 292) is: "Nobody knows, and you can't find out".

OK. If this is so, why bother? Because *Afterwords* takes the mystery of language and puts it right back into its own mystery; that is, *Afterwords* ex-plains the mystery of language by taking language *out* ("ex-") of the plane of its mystery, so as to become visible to all before it slips back into its plane. This in itself is a remarkable achievement that has been denied to almost all linguists, for they stick to the description of the plane without seeing that it is the plane that holds their descriptions.

Consider the proposition "There is food at 200 yards due east." This is a declarative sentence with a qualifying clause in English which when translated, for instance, into Bee will be easily understood by bees. Consider now the proposition "This is a declarative sentence with a qualifying clause." This is a proposition upon a proposition in a language that speaks about language. Call this a "second-order language", or "meta-language" or short. Propositions in meta-language cannot be translated into Bee.

The topology of a nervous system that understands and speaks meta-language must close on itself in a particular way. The bees don't have it. It is doubtful whether metalinguistic propositions can be made in any other animal language but Homo. Be this as it may, the blessed curse of a meta-language is that it wears the cloth of a first-order language, an "object language". Thus any proposition carries with it the tantalizing ambiguity: Was it made in meta- or in object-language? Nobody knows, and you can't find out. All attempts to speak *about* a meta-language, that is, to speak *in* meta-metalanguage, are doomed to fail, as Wittgenstein observed: "Remain silent!"

Brockman undooms the doom by an existential undoing of what was left undone. "Existential," for any Beginning is *not* to follow; that is, to begin is first to undo; then one has to undo the beginning in order to begin, and so on.

*   *   *

Intrigued, one follows the construction of Brockman's formidable machinery for doing the undoing, whose cogwheels, levers, pegs, interlocks, springs, etc., are anatomy, anthropology, architecture, astrophysics, biology, cybernetics, epistemology, heuristics, iconography, linguistics, logic, magic, metaphysics, neurophysiology, neuropsychiatry, philosophy, physics, physiology, poetry, proxemics, psychology, quantum mechanics, relativity, zoology, etc. to name a few.

All who are concerned about the violence committed in the name of language will appreciate the useful uselessness of Brockman's un-book.